WORLD'S FASTEST TRAINS

By Brienna Rossiter

WWW.APEXEDITIONS.COM

Apex is distributed by North Star Editions:
sales@northstareditions.com | 888-417-0195

Produced for Apex by Red Line Editorial.

Photographs ©: Tetsuya Nakamura/Yomiuri Shimbun/AP Images, cover, 1; Shutterstock Images, 4–5, 6–7, 8, 9, 10–11, 12, 13, 14, 15, 16–17, 18–19, 20, 21, 22–23, 24–25, 26, 29; iStockphoto, 27

Library of Congress Control Number: 2021918401

ISBN
978-1-63738-174-8 (hardcover)
978-1-63738-210-3 (paperback)
978-1-63738-278-3 (ebook pdf)
978-1-63738-246-2 (hosted ebook)

Printed in the United States of America
Mankato, MN
012022

NOTE TO PARENTS AND EDUCATORS

Apex books are designed to build literacy skills in striving readers. Exciting, high-interest content attracts and holds readers' attention. The text is carefully leveled to allow students to achieve success quickly. Additional features, such as bolded glossary words for difficult terms, help build comprehension.

TABLE OF CONTENTS

CHAPTER 1

ON THE FAST TRACK

A train zooms through Shanghai, China. The train has no wheels. Instead, it floats just above the track.

The Shanghai Maglev is much quieter than regular trains.

Powerful magnets make the train move. It goes 268 miles per hour (431 km/h).

A maglev train uses two sets of magnets. One set is on the bottom of the train. The other set lies on the track.

MAGLEV TRAINS

Magnets create a **charge** between a **maglev** train and its track. They make the train speed up or slow down. Without wheels, maglev trains have less **friction**. So, they can go much faster than other trains.

The train carries people from Shanghai to the airport. This trip is 19 miles (31 km) long. But it takes just eight minutes.

Many people take the Shanghai Maglev after landing in the city's airport.

About 27 million people lived in Shanghai in 2021. It is one of the world's largest cities.

The Shanghai Maglev began running in 2003. It's still one of the world's fastest trains.

HIGH-SPEED HISTORY

The first **high-speed train** opened in 1964. It connected two cities in Japan. Japan soon added trains to other cities.

Japan's first high-speed train ran between Tokyo and Osaka. It passed by Mount Fuji.

Some of Japan's trains today go 186 miles per hour (300 km/h).

Japan's fast trains were known as "bullet trains." They could go 130 miles per hour (210 km/h). France made a high-speed train in the 1980s. It went 168 miles per hour (270 km/h).

A second French train used a flatter track. This allowed it to go even faster.

France's high-speed train line is known as the Train à Grande Vitesse, or TGV.

By the 2000s, several countries in Europe and Asia had high-speed trains. Many went more than 200 miles per hour (322 km/h).

High-speed trains are often commuter trains. They carry hundreds of passengers within and between busy cities.

South Korea built its first high-speed train in 2004. The Korail KTX has a top speed of 205 miles per hour (330 km/h).

TRAIN TRAVEL

High-speed trains connect major cities across Europe. Riding these trains can be faster than traveling by airplane. It also costs less.

CHAPTER 3

ELECTRIC TRAINS

F rance's TGV POS set the record for speed in 2007. The train went 357 miles per hour (575 km/h).

The TGV POS is an electric train. It usually goes 200 miles per hour (322 km/h).

Many of the fastest trains are in China.

These trains run on special tracks.

China's train stations often have lots of high-speed trains to choose from.

China has the world's largest high-speed rail network.

CUTTING COSTS

Building new tracks for high-speed trains costs a lot. Fuel can be expensive, too. So, many trains use electric **batteries**. These trains can often use old tracks. They also require less fuel.

The Fuxing Hao can go from Beijing to Shanghai in five hours. That's half the time it would take a regular train.

The Fuxing Hao runs from Beijing to Shanghai. It can go 220 miles per hour (354 km/h). The CRH380A is even faster. It carries passengers at 236 miles per hour (380 km/h).

One Fuxing Hao train can carry 556 passengers.

The CRH380A once reached 302 miles per hour (486 km/h) during testing.

CHAPTER 4

OTHER FUELS

In 2021, the Shanghai Maglev was still the fastest maglev train. But Japan began testing the L0 Series in 2013. One of its maglev trains reached 374 miles per hour (602 km/h) in 2015.

LO Series trains were still being tested in 2021. Passengers couldn't ride them yet.

The fastest diesel train was the InterCity 125. This train went 148 miles per hour (238 km/h) in 1987.

The InterCity 125 was named for its usual speed in miles per hour.

InterCity 125 trains ran in the United Kingdom from 1976 until 2021.

However, diesel fuel harms the **environment**. So, people are exploring other ways to make fast trains. Many trains are **hybrids**. They use less fuel.

A hybrid train replaced the InterCity 125. This new train can partly recharge its electric batteries when it brakes.

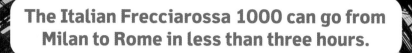
The Italian Frecciarossa 1000 can go from Milan to Rome in less than three hours.

FAST AND EARTH-FRIENDLY

The Frecciarossa 1000 connects cities in Europe. This train has a top speed of 249 miles per hour (400 km/h). It's also Earth-friendly. It's mostly made from **renewable** materials.

COMPREHENSION QUESTIONS

Write your answers on a separate piece of paper.

1. Write a sentence describing how a maglev train works.

2. Would you want to ride a high-speed train? Why or why not?

3. Which country built the first high-speed train?

    A. Japan

    B. China

    C. France

4. Why would a flat track help a train go faster?

    A. The train wouldn't lose speed when going up slopes.

    B. The train wouldn't need a driver.

    C. The train would never need to stop.

5. What does **expensive** mean in this book?

*Building new tracks for high-speed trains costs a lot. Fuel can be **expensive**, too.*

> **A.** having a high price
> **B.** having a low price
> **C.** having the wrong shape

6. What does **require** mean in this book?

*These trains can often use old tracks. They also **require** less fuel.*

> **A.** to spend money
> **B.** to need something
> **C.** to break something

Answer key on page 32.

GLOSSARY

batteries
Devices that store energy, often used to power machines.

charge
A force related to electricity that can cause objects to stay together or push apart.

environment
The natural surroundings of living things.

friction
A force that happens when objects rub against one another, often slowing them down.

high-speed train
A train that moves very fast, often more than 124 miles per hour (200 km/h).

hybrids
Machines that can use two different sources of energy.

maglev
Short for "magnetic levitation." It refers to a train that floats above a track and is moved by magnets.

network
A large group of things that are connected together.

renewable
Possible to get or make more of, so it will not run out.

TO LEARN MORE

BOOKS

Croft, Debbie. *High-Speed Trains.* New York: Houghton Mifflin Harcourt, 2019.

Hamilton, S. L. *The World's Fastest Trains*. Minneapolis: Abdo Publishing, 2021.

Wood, John. *Travel Technology: Maglev Trains, Hovercrafts, and More*. New York: Gareth Stevens Publishing, 2019.

ONLINE RESOURCES

Visit **www.apexeditions.com** to find links and resources related to this title.

ABOUT THE AUTHOR

Brienna Rossiter is a writer and editor who lives in Minnesota. She enjoys reading about animals and science.

INDEX

Answer Key:
1. Answers will vary; 2. Answers will vary; 3. A; 4. A; 5. A; 6. B